WALTER THE EDUCATOR'S LITTLE BBQ RECIPES COOKBOOK

Walter the Educator's Little BBQ Recipes Cookbook

Walter the Educator

Silent King Books a WhichHead Imprint

Copyright © 2024 by Walter the Educator

All rights reserved. No part of this book may be reproduced in any manner whatsoever without written permission except in the case of brief quotations embodied in critical articles and reviews.

First Printing, 2024

Disclaimer
This book is for entertainment and informational purposes only. The author and publisher offer this information without warranties expressed or implied. No matter the grounds, neither the author nor the publisher will be accountable for any losses, injuries, or other damages caused by the reader's use of this book. The use of this book acknowledges an understanding and acceptance of this disclaimer.

dedicated to all those that enjoy great food

CONTENTS

Dedication v

One - Walter's Barbecue Chicken Pizza 1

Two - Walter's Barbecue Sweet And Tangy Sauce 3

Three - Walter's Barbecue Oven Chicken . . 5

Four - Walter's Barbecue Pork Chops . . . 7

Five - Walter's Grilled Picante Barbecue Chicken 9

Six - Walter's Korean Barbecue Experience 11

Seven - Walter's Barbecue Potato Roast . . 14

Eight - Walter's Sweet And Spicy Barbecue Chicken 16

Nine - Walter's Unique Barbecue Sauce . . 18

Ten - Walter's Barbecue Salmon 20

Eleven - Walter's Smoky Tender Steak 22

Twelve - Walter's Barbecue Turkey 24

Thirteen - Walter's Barbecue Vegetables . . 26

Fourteen - Walter's Barbecue Burgers . . . 28

Fifteen - Walter's Barbecue Sausages . . . 30

Sixteen - Walter's Grilled Aussie Lamb Chops 32

Seventeen - Walter's Barbecue Kabobs . . . 34

Eighteen - Walter's Barbecue Baby Back Ribs 36

Nineteen - Walter's Barbecue Meatballs . . 38

Twenty - Walter's Barbecue-infused Smoky Cheddar Bread 40

Twenty-One - Walter's Barbecue Fish 42

Twenty-Two - Walter's Caribbean Jerk BBQ Chicken 44

Twenty-Three - Walter's Barbecue Dry Rub 47

Twenty-Four - Walter's Barbecue Corn . . . 49

Twenty-Five - Walter's Barbecue Brisket . . 51

Twenty-Six - Walter's Barbecue Chicken Tenders 54

Twenty-Seven - Walter's Barbecue Eggplant With Mint And Feta 56

Twenty-Eight - Walter's Barbecue Bacon Wraps 58

Twenty-Nine - Walter's Barbecue Seafood Skewers 60

About The Author 62

ONE

WALTER'S BARBECUE CHICKEN PIZZA

Ingredients:
1 pound pizza dough
1 cup barbecue sauce
1 cup shredded cooked chicken
1/2 red onion, thinly sliced
1 cup shredded mozzarella cheese
1/2 cup fresh cilantro, chopped
1/4 cup cornmeal (for dusting)
Steps:
Preheat your oven to 450°F (230°C).
Dust a baking sheet with cornmeal to prevent sticking, then roll out the pizza dough to your desired thickness and shape.
Spread the barbecue sauce evenly over the pizza dough, leaving a small border around the edges.

Sprinkle the shredded chicken and sliced red onion over the sauce.

Top with the shredded mozzarella cheese.

Transfer the pizza to the preheated oven and bake for 12-15 minutes, or until the crust is golden and the cheese is bubbly.

Once the pizza is out of the oven, sprinkle the chopped cilantro over the top for a burst of fresh flavor.

Slice the pizza, serve, and enjoy your unique and delicious barbecue chicken pizza!

This recipe offers a delightful blend of tangy barbecue sauce, tender chicken, and the freshness of cilantro, making it a mouthwatering twist on a classic pizza.

TWO

WALTER'S BARBECUE SWEET AND TANGY SAUCE

Ingredients:
1 cup ketchup
1/2 cup apple cider vinegar
1/4 cup brown sugar
2 tablespoons honey
1 tablespoon Worcestershire sauce
1 tablespoon Dijon mustard
1 teaspoon smoked paprika
1 teaspoon garlic powder
1/2 teaspoon onion powder
1/2 teaspoon cayenne pepper
Salt and black pepper to taste
Steps:

In a medium saucepan, combine the ketchup, apple cider vinegar, brown sugar, honey, Worcestershire sauce, and Dijon mustard.

Place the saucepan over medium heat and stir to combine the ingredients.

Add the smoked paprika, garlic powder, onion powder, and cayenne pepper to the saucepan, stirring well to incorporate the flavors.

Season the sauce with salt and black pepper to taste, adjusting the seasoning as needed.

Allow the sauce to simmer over low heat for 15-20 minutes, stirring occasionally, until it thickens to your desired consistency.

Once the barbecue sweet and tangy sauce reaches the perfect thickness, remove it from the heat and let it cool slightly.

Transfer the sauce to a jar or airtight container for storage, and refrigerate until ready to use.

Use this unique and flavorful barbecue sweet and tangy sauce to elevate your grilled chicken, ribs, or pulled pork with its irresistible blend of sweet, tangy, and smoky flavors.

This recipe offers a harmonious fusion of sweet and tangy notes, complemented by the warmth of spices, making it a standout addition to your barbecue repertoire.

THREE

WALTER'S BARBECUE OVEN CHICKEN

Ingredients:
4 bone-in chicken thighs
4 bone-in chicken drumsticks
1 cup barbecue sauce
2 tablespoons olive oil
1 tablespoon smoked paprika
1 tablespoon garlic powder
1 tablespoon onion powder
1 teaspoon cayenne pepper
Salt and black pepper to taste
Fresh parsley for garnish
Steps:
Preheat your oven to 375°F (190°C).
In a small bowl, mix together the olive oil, smoked paprika, garlic powder, onion powder, cayenne pepper,

salt, and black pepper to create a flavorful marinade.

Place the chicken thighs and drumsticks in a large bowl, then rub the marinade all over the chicken pieces, ensuring they are evenly coated.

Arrange the chicken in a single layer on a baking sheet lined with parchment paper or aluminum foil.

Transfer the baking sheet to the preheated oven and bake the chicken for 25 minutes.

After 25 minutes, remove the chicken from the oven and generously brush each piece with barbecue sauce.

Return the chicken to the oven and continue baking for an additional 15-20 minutes, or until the chicken is cooked through and the barbecue sauce has caramelized.

Once the chicken is done, remove it from the oven and let it rest for a few minutes.

Garnish the barbecue oven chicken with freshly chopped parsley for a touch of freshness and color.

Serve the succulent barbecue oven chicken alongside your favorite sides and enjoy the irresistible combination of tender, flavorful meat with a caramelized barbecue glaze.

This recipe promises tender, juicy chicken infused with a smoky, tangy barbecue flavor, making it a delightful and hassle-free option for a satisfying meal straight from your oven.

FOUR

WALTER'S BARBECUE PORK CHOPS

Ingredients:
4 bone-in pork chops
1/4 cup honey
1/4 cup barbecue sauce
2 tablespoons soy sauce
2 cloves garlic, minced
1 teaspoon Dijon mustard
1 teaspoon paprika
1/2 teaspoon ground cumin
Salt and black pepper to taste
Fresh parsley for garnish
Steps:

In a small bowl, whisk together the honey, barbecue sauce, soy sauce, minced garlic, Dijon mustard, paprika, ground cumin, salt, and black pepper to create a luscious marinade.

Place the pork chops in a shallow dish and pour the marinade over them, ensuring they are well coated.

Cover the dish and refrigerate for at least 30 minutes to allow the flavors to meld.

Preheat your grill to medium-high heat, then lightly oil the grate.

Remove the pork chops from the marinade, allowing any excess marinade to drip off.

Grill the pork chops for 5-7 minutes on each side, or until they are cooked through and have beautiful grill marks.

While grilling, baste the pork chops with the remaining marinade to build up a sticky, flavorful glaze.

Once the pork chops are cooked to your desired doneness, remove them from the grill and let them rest for a few minutes.

Garnish the honey barbecue pork chops with freshly chopped parsley for a burst of color and freshness.

Serve the succulent pork chops alongside your favorite sides and savor the delectable combination of tender meat with a sweet and tangy barbecue glaze.

This recipe offers a delightful balance of sweet, savory, and smoky flavors, resulting in tender and juicy pork chops that are sure to impress your taste buds.

FIVE

WALTER'S GRILLED PICANTE BARBECUE CHICKEN

Ingredients:
4 boneless, skinless chicken breasts
1 cup picante sauce
1/4 cup barbecue sauce
Salt and pepper to taste
Steps:
In a bowl, mix the picante sauce and barbecue sauce together. Set aside half of the mixture to serve with the chicken later.

Season the chicken breasts with salt and pepper, then place them in a resealable plastic bag or a shallow dish.

Pour the remaining picante sauce mixture over the

chicken, ensuring it is well coated. Marinate the chicken in the refrigerator for at least 4 hours, or preferably overnight for maximum flavor infusion.

Preheat your grill to medium heat and lightly oil the grill rack to prevent sticking.

Remove the chicken from the marinade and discard the used marinade.

Place the chicken on the grill and cook for about 15 minutes, turning and basting often with the reserved picante barbecue sauce mixture, until the chicken is cooked through and the exterior is nicely caramelized.

Once the chicken is done, remove it from the grill and let it rest for a few minutes.

Serve the succulent grilled picante barbecue chicken with the reserved picante sauce mixture on the side for dipping.

Enjoy the zesty and flavorful grilled picante barbecue chicken, perfect for a delightful meal with a hint of spice and tanginess.

SIX

WALTER'S KOREAN BARBECUE EXPERIENCE

Ingredients:
1.5 lbs (680g) thinly sliced beef (such as ribeye or sirloin)
1/2 cup soy sauce
1/4 cup brown sugar
2 tablespoons sesame oil
4 cloves garlic, minced
1 tablespoon grated ginger
2 tablespoons rice vinegar
2 tablespoons mirin
1 tablespoon gochujang (Korean chili paste)
1/2 teaspoon black pepper
4 green onions, thinly sliced

1 tablespoon toasted sesame seeds

Optional: Sliced carrots, onions, and mushrooms for grilling

Steps:

In a bowl, whisk together soy sauce, brown sugar, sesame oil, garlic, ginger, rice vinegar, mirin, gochujang, and black pepper to create the marinade.

Place the thinly sliced beef in a shallow dish or resealable plastic bag and pour the marinade over the beef, ensuring it is well coated. Add the sliced green onions and mix well. Marinate the beef in the refrigerator for at least 2 hours, allowing the flavors to infuse.

Preheat the grill to medium-high heat. If using vegetables, you can thread them onto skewers or use a grilling basket.

Remove the beef from the marinade, allowing any excess marinade to drip off.

Grill the beef for 2-3 minutes on each side, or until it is cooked to your desired doneness and has a charred exterior.

If using vegetables, grill them until they are tender and slightly charred.

Once the beef and vegetables are done, arrange them on a serving platter and sprinkle with toasted sesame seeds.

Serve the Korean barbecue beef and vegetables with steamed rice, kimchi, and other banchan (side dishes) for a complete and authentic Korean dining experience.

This recipe offers a tantalizing blend of savory, sweet, and spicy flavors, delivering a mouthwatering Korean barbecue experience that's perfect for a special meal or gathering.

SEVEN

WALTER'S BARBECUE POTATO ROAST

Ingredients:
4 large potatoes, thinly sliced
1 onion, thinly sliced
3 cloves of garlic, minced
1/4 cup olive oil
2 tablespoons barbecue seasoning
Salt and pepper to taste
Fresh parsley for garnish
Steps:

Preheat the oven to 375°F (190°C) and lightly grease a baking dish.

In a large bowl, combine the thinly sliced potatoes, sliced onion, minced garlic, olive oil, barbecue seasoning, salt, and pepper. Toss until the potatoes and onions are evenly coated with the seasoning and oil mixture.

Arrange the seasoned potato and onion slices in the prepared baking dish, layering them evenly.

Cover the baking dish with foil and place it in the preheated oven.

Roast the potatoes for 30 minutes, then remove the foil and continue roasting for an additional 15-20 minutes, or until the potatoes are tender and golden brown.

Once the barbecue potato roast is done, remove it from the oven and let it rest for a few minutes.

Garnish the roasted potatoes with fresh parsley for a burst of color and freshness.

Serve the flavorful barbecue potato roast as a delicious side dish or as a standalone vegetarian option, perfect for any meal or gathering.

EIGHT

WALTER'S SWEET AND SPICY BARBECUE CHICKEN

Ingredients:
2 lbs chicken thighs, skin-on
1 cup barbecue sauce
1/4 cup honey
2 tablespoons soy sauce
1 tablespoon hot sauce
2 cloves garlic, minced
1 teaspoon paprika
1/2 teaspoon cayenne pepper
Salt and pepper to taste
Steps:

In a bowl, whisk together the barbecue sauce, honey, soy sauce, hot sauce, minced garlic, paprika, cayenne pepper, salt, and pepper to create the sweet and spicy barbecue marinade.

Place the chicken thighs in a resealable plastic bag or a shallow dish, and pour the marinade over the chicken, ensuring it's well-coated. Marinate in the refrigerator for at least 2 hours or overnight for maximum flavor.

Preheat the grill to medium-high heat.

Remove the chicken from the marinade, letting any excess drip off.

Place the chicken on the grill and cook for 6-7 minutes on each side, basting with the remaining marinade to build a sticky, flavorful glaze.

Once the chicken is cooked through and has a caramelized exterior, remove it from the grill and let it rest for a few minutes.

Garnish the sweet and spicy barbecue chicken with chopped green onions for a pop of color and freshness.

Serve the succulent sweet and spicy barbecue chicken alongside your favorite sides and savor the irresistible combination of tender, flavorful meat with a perfect balance of sweet and spicy notes.

This recipe offers a delightful combination of sweet and heat, resulting in succulent, flavorful chicken that's perfect for grilling season.

NINE

WALTER'S UNIQUE BARBECUE SAUCE

Ingredients:
1 cup ketchup
1/2 cup apple cider vinegar
1/4 cup honey
2 tablespoons molasses
1 tablespoon Worcestershire sauce
1 teaspoon smoked paprika
1 teaspoon garlic powder
1 teaspoon onion powder
1/2 teaspoon cayenne pepper
Salt and black pepper to taste
Steps:

In a saucepan over medium heat, combine the ketchup, apple cider vinegar, honey, and molasses. Stir in the Worcestershire sauce, smoked paprika, garlic powder, onion powder, and cayenne pepper.

Season the mixture with a pinch of salt and black pepper.

Bring the sauce to a gentle simmer, then reduce the heat and let it cook for 15-20 minutes, stirring occasionally, until the flavors meld and the sauce thickens to your desired consistency.

Once the barbecue sauce reaches the perfect thickness, remove it from the heat and let it cool slightly.

Transfer the sauce to a jar or airtight container for storage, and refrigerate until ready to use.

Use this unique and flavorful barbecue sauce to elevate your grilled meats, sandwiches, and more with its irresistible blend of sweet, tangy, and smoky flavors.

This recipe offers a harmonious fusion of sweet, tangy, and smoky elements, making it a standout addition to your barbecue repertoire.

TEN

WALTER'S BARBECUE SALMON

Ingredients:
4 salmon fillets
1/2 cup barbecue sauce
2 tablespoons honey
1 tablespoon soy sauce
1 teaspoon minced garlic
1 teaspoon paprika
Salt and pepper to taste
Fresh lemon wedges for serving

Steps:

Preheat the grill to medium-high heat and lightly oil the grates to prevent sticking.

In a small bowl, mix together the barbecue sauce, honey, soy sauce, minced garlic, paprika, salt, and pepper to create the marinade.

Place the salmon fillets in a shallow dish and pour the marinade over the top, ensuring each fillet is coated evenly. Let the salmon marinate for 15-20 minutes.

Once marinated, place the salmon fillets on the grill and cook for 4-5 minutes per side, basting with the remaining marinade to create a caramelized glaze.

Once the salmon is cooked through and has a slightly charred exterior, remove it from the grill.

Serve the barbecue salmon with fresh lemon wedges for a bright, citrusy finish.

Enjoy the succulent and flavorful barbecue salmon with a perfect balance of sweet, tangy, and smoky flavors.

ELEVEN

WALTER'S SMOKY TENDER STEAK

Ingredients:
4 beef steaks (such as ribeye or sirloin)
1/2 cup barbecue sauce
2 tablespoons olive oil
2 cloves garlic, minced
1 teaspoon paprika
1 teaspoon onion powder
Salt and pepper to taste
Steps:

In a small bowl, mix together the barbecue sauce, olive oil, minced garlic, paprika, and onion powder to create a marinade.

Season the steaks with salt and pepper, then place them in a shallow dish or resealable plastic bag.

Pour the marinade over the steaks, ensuring they are

evenly coated. Cover the dish or seal the bag, then refrigerate for at least 2 hours, or overnight for maximum flavor.

Preheat the grill to medium-high heat.

Remove the steaks from the marinade and discard any excess marinade.

Grill the steaks for 4-5 minutes on each side, or to your preferred level of doneness, basting with additional barbecue sauce during the last few minutes of grilling.

Once the steaks are cooked to your liking, transfer them to a plate and let them rest for a few minutes.

Slice the steaks against the grain and serve with your favorite barbecue sides for a delicious and satisfying meal.

This recipe results in tender, juicy steaks infused with smoky barbecue flavor, making it a fantastic option for a flavorful and satisfying dinner.

TWELVE

WALTER'S BARBECUE TURKEY

Ingredients:
1 whole turkey, about 12-14 pounds
1/4 cup olive oil
1 tablespoon smoked paprika
1 tablespoon garlic powder
1 tablespoon onion powder
1 teaspoon cayenne pepper
1 teaspoon ground cumin
Salt and black pepper to taste
2 cups barbecue sauce

Steps:

Preheat your grill to medium-high heat, around 375-400°F (190-200°C).

In a small bowl, mix together the olive oil, smoked paprika, garlic powder, onion powder, cayenne pepper, ground cumin, salt, and black pepper to create a flavorful rub.

Pat the turkey dry with paper towels and brush the entire surface with the prepared spice rub.

Place the turkey on the grill, breast side up, and close the lid. Grill the turkey for about 2-2.5 hours, or until the internal temperature reaches 165°F (74°C), basting with barbecue sauce every 30 minutes.

Once the turkey is cooked through, carefully transfer it to a cutting board and let it rest for 20-30 minutes before carving.

Carve the turkey and serve with additional barbecue sauce on the side for extra flavor.

This recipe yields a succulent and flavorful barbecue turkey with a smoky, spicy kick, perfect for a festive and delicious holiday meal or any special occasion.

THIRTEEN

WALTER'S BARBECUE VEGETABLES

Ingredients:
Assorted vegetables (such as bell peppers, zucchini, red onion, mushrooms, and cherry tomatoes)
Olive oil
Salt and pepper
Barbecue seasoning
Steps:
Preheat the grill to medium-high heat.
Wash and prepare the vegetables, cutting them into even-sized pieces.
In a bowl, toss the vegetables with olive oil, salt, pepper, and barbecue seasoning to coat evenly.
Place the seasoned vegetables on a grill pan or skewers, ensuring they are spread out to allow for even cooking.

Grill the vegetables for 8-10 minutes, turning occasionally, until they are slightly charred and tender.

Once the vegetables are cooked to your liking, remove them from the grill.

Transfer the grilled vegetables to a serving platter and garnish with fresh herbs or a drizzle of balsamic glaze for extra flavor.

Serve the barbecue vegetables as a delicious and vibrant side dish or as a vegetarian main course option.

This recipe offers a delightful way to enjoy the natural flavors of assorted vegetables enhanced with a smoky barbecue seasoning, making it a perfect addition to any outdoor gathering or as a flavorful accompaniment to grilled meats.

FOURTEEN

WALTER'S BARBECUE BURGERS

Ingredients:
1 pound ground beef
1/2 cup barbecue sauce
1 teaspoon garlic powder
1 teaspoon onion powder
Salt and pepper to taste
4 burger buns
Lettuce, tomato, onion, and other desired toppings
Steps:
In a bowl, mix the ground beef with the barbecue sauce, garlic powder, onion powder, salt, and pepper until well combined.
Divide the beef mixture into 4 equal portions and shape them into burger patties.
Preheat the grill or a skillet over medium-high heat.

Cook the burger patties for about 4-5 minutes on each side, or until they reach your desired level of doneness, basting with additional barbecue sauce while cooking.

Toast the burger buns on the grill or in a toaster until lightly golden.

Assemble the burgers by placing the cooked patties on the buns and topping them with lettuce, tomato, onion, and any other desired toppings.

Serve the barbecue burgers alongside your favorite sides and enjoy the smoky, savory flavors in each delicious bite.

This recipe yields juicy and flavorful barbecue burgers with a perfect balance of smokiness and sweetness, making them a delightful option for a satisfying meal.

FIFTEEN

WALTER'S BARBECUE SAUSAGES

Ingredients:

1 pound of your favorite sausages (such as bratwurst, Italian, or chorizo)

1/2 cup barbecue sauce

1 tablespoon olive oil

1 teaspoon smoked paprika

1/2 teaspoon garlic powder

Salt and pepper to taste

Optional: sliced onions and bell peppers for serving

Steps:

Preheat the grill to medium-high heat.

In a small bowl, mix together the barbecue sauce, olive oil, smoked paprika, garlic powder, salt, and pepper to create a flavorful marinade.

Place the sausages in a large resealable plastic bag

or a shallow dish, and pour the marinade over them, ensuring they are evenly coated. Let the sausages marinate for at least 30 minutes to allow the flavors to infuse.

Once the sausages have marinated, remove them from the bag or dish and place them on the preheated grill. If desired, you can also grill the sliced onions and bell peppers alongside the sausages for a delicious addition.

Grill the sausages for 10-15 minutes, turning occasionally and basting with any remaining marinade, until they are cooked through and have a slight char.

Once the sausages are grilled to perfection, remove them from the grill and let them rest for a few minutes.

Serve the barbecue sausages with the grilled onions and bell peppers, if using, and enjoy the smoky, savory flavors of this mouthwatering dish.

This recipe offers a delightful twist to traditional grilled sausages, infusing them with a rich barbecue flavor that will surely be a hit at any cookout or gathering.

SIXTEEN

WALTER'S GRILLED AUSSIE LAMB CHOPS

Ingredients:
8 pieces of Australian lamb chops
1/3 cup soy sauce
1/4 cup red wine
2 cloves of garlic, crushed
2 teaspoons grated fresh ginger
2 tablespoons brown sugar
1 tablespoon barbecue sauce
Salt and pepper to taste
Fresh rosemary sprigs for garnish
Instructions:
In a bowl, mix together soy sauce, red wine, crushed garlic, grated ginger, brown sugar, and barbecue sauce to create the marinade.
Place the lamb chops in a shallow dish and pour

the marinade over them, ensuring each piece is well coated. Cover the dish and refrigerate for at least 2 hours, or preferably overnight, to let the flavors infuse.

Preheat the barbecue grill to medium-high heat.

Remove the lamb chops from the marinade and season with salt and pepper.

Grill the lamb chops for about 3-4 minutes on each side, or to your desired level of doneness, basting with the remaining marinade during the grilling process.

Once the lamb chops are cooked to perfection, transfer them to a serving platter and garnish with fresh rosemary sprigs for a fragrant touch.

Serve the succulent grilled Aussie lamb chops with your favorite barbecue sides and enjoy the delicious flavors of an Australian-inspired barbecue feast.

This recipe captures the essence of Australian barbecue by showcasing the rich flavors of marinated lamb chops grilled to perfection, making it a delightful addition to any outdoor gathering or barbecue event.

SEVENTEEN

WALTER'S BARBECUE KABOBS

Ingredients:
1 pound of beef sirloin, cut into cubes
1 pound of chicken breast, cut into cubes
1 red bell pepper, cut into chunks
1 green bell pepper, cut into chunks
1 red onion, cut into chunks
8 oz of mushrooms
Wooden skewers, soaked in water for 30 minutes
Marinade:
1/4 cup soy sauce
2 tablespoons honey
2 tablespoons olive oil
2 cloves garlic, minced
1 teaspoon paprika
1 teaspoon cumin

Salt and pepper to taste

Steps:

In a bowl, combine the soy sauce, honey, olive oil, minced garlic, paprika, cumin, salt, and pepper to create the marinade.

Place the beef cubes in one resealable plastic bag and the chicken cubes in another. Divide the marinade evenly between the two bags, ensuring the meat is coated. Seal the bags and refrigerate for at least 1 hour, or overnight for best flavor.

Preheat the grill to medium-high heat.

Thread the marinated beef, chicken, bell peppers, red onion, and mushrooms onto the soaked wooden skewers, alternating the ingredients as desired.

Grill the kabobs for about 10-12 minutes, turning occasionally, until the meat is cooked through and the vegetables are charred and tender.

Once done, remove the kabobs from the grill and let them rest for a few minutes.

Serve the flavorful barbecue kabobs with a side of rice, salad, or your favorite dipping sauce for a delicious and satisfying meal. Enjoy the succulent, smoky flavors of these marinated kabobs!

EIGHTEEN

WALTER'S BARBECUE BABY BACK RIBS

Ingredients:
2 racks of baby back ribs
1 cup of your favorite barbecue sauce
1/4 cup brown sugar
2 tablespoons paprika
1 tablespoon garlic powder
1 tablespoon onion powder
1 teaspoon cayenne pepper
Salt and black pepper to taste

Steps:

Preheat your grill to medium heat, around 275-300°F (135-150°C).

In a bowl, mix together the brown sugar, paprika, garlic powder, onion powder, cayenne pepper, salt, and black pepper to create a dry rub.

Pat the baby back ribs dry with paper towels, then generously rub the dry spice mixture all over the ribs, covering both sides.

Place the ribs on the grill, bone side down, and cook for 2-2.5 hours, using indirect heat by turning off the burners directly under the ribs and maintaining the temperature around 275-300°F (135-150°C).

During the last 30 minutes of cooking, baste the ribs with your favorite barbecue sauce, allowing it to caramelize and create a flavorful glaze.

Once the ribs are tender and the meat has shrunk back from the bones, remove them from the grill and let them rest for a few minutes.

Slice the ribs between the bones and serve with extra barbecue sauce on the side for dipping.

Enjoy the tender, smoky, and succulent barbecue baby back ribs with your favorite sides for a delicious and satisfying meal.

This recipe results in perfectly cooked baby back ribs with a flavorful dry rub and a caramelized barbecue glaze, making them a standout dish for any barbecue gathering or special occasion.

NINETEEN

WALTER'S BARBECUE MEATBALLS

Ingredients:
1 pound ground beef
1/2 cup breadcrumbs
1/4 cup grated parmesan cheese
1/4 cup chopped parsley
1 egg
1 teaspoon garlic powder
1 teaspoon onion powder
Salt and pepper to taste
1 cup barbecue sauce

Steps:

Preheat the grill to medium-high heat.

In a mixing bowl, combine the ground beef, breadcrumbs, parmesan cheese, parsley, egg, garlic powder, onion powder, salt, and pepper. Mix until well combined.

Shape the mixture into meatballs, about 1 to 1.5 inches in diameter.

Place the meatballs on the preheated grill and cook for 12-15 minutes, turning occasionally, until they are browned and cooked through.

In a small saucepan, warm the barbecue sauce over medium heat.

Once the meatballs are cooked, brush them with the warm barbecue sauce or toss them in a bowl with the sauce to coat evenly.

Serve the barbecue meatballs as an appetizer, over pasta, or as a main dish, garnished with additional chopped parsley if desired.

These barbecue meatballs are a savory and flavorful twist on a classic dish, perfect for gatherings or as a hearty meal option.

TWENTY

WALTER'S BARBECUE-INFUSED SMOKY CHEDDAR BREAD

Ingredients:
3 cups all-purpose flour
1 tablespoon baking powder
1 teaspoon salt
1/4 cup granulated sugar
1/4 cup barbecue sauce
1 cup grated smoky cheddar cheese
1/4 cup diced red onions
1/4 cup chopped fresh parsley
1 1/4 cups milk
1/4 cup vegetable oil

1 egg

Steps:

Preheat your oven to 375°F (190°C) and grease a 9x5-inch loaf pan.

In a large bowl, combine the flour, baking powder, salt, and sugar.

In a separate bowl, mix the barbecue sauce, grated smoky cheddar cheese, diced red onions, and chopped fresh parsley.

In another bowl, whisk together the milk, vegetable oil, and egg.

Add the wet ingredients to the dry ingredients, stirring until just combined. Fold in the barbecue sauce and cheese mixture until evenly distributed.

Pour the batter into the prepared loaf pan and smooth the top.

Bake for 45-50 minutes or until a toothpick inserted into the center comes out clean.

Allow the bread to cool in the pan for 10 minutes, then transfer it to a wire rack to cool completely.

This unique barbecue-infused smoky cheddar bread offers a delightful combination of savory and smoky flavors, making it a perfect addition to a barbecue gathering or as a standalone snack.

TWENTY-ONE

WALTER'S BARBECUE FISH

Ingredients:

4 fillets of your choice of fish (such as salmon, trout, or tilapia)

1/4 cup barbecue sauce

2 tablespoons olive oil

1 teaspoon smoked paprika

1 teaspoon garlic powder

Salt and pepper to taste

Lemon wedges for serving

Fresh parsley for garnish

Steps:

Preheat the grill to medium-high heat and lightly oil the grate to prevent sticking.

In a small bowl, mix the barbecue sauce, olive oil, smoked paprika, garlic powder, salt, and pepper to create a marinade.

Place the fish fillets in a shallow dish and coat them with the marinade, ensuring that each fillet is evenly covered. Let the fish marinate for 15-20 minutes.

Once the fish has marinated, place the fillets on the preheated grill. Cook for 4-5 minutes on each side, or until the fish is cooked through and has grill marks.

Carefully remove the fish from the grill and transfer to a serving platter.

Squeeze fresh lemon juice over the grilled fish and garnish with chopped parsley.

Serve the barbecue fish alongside your favorite side dishes and enjoy the smoky, savory flavors of this delicious seafood dish.

This recipe offers a delightful way to enjoy the natural flavors of fish enhanced with a smoky barbecue seasoning, making it a perfect addition to any outdoor gathering or as a flavorful main course option.

TWENTY-TWO

WALTER'S CARIBBEAN JERK BBQ CHICKEN

Ingredients:
4 bone-in chicken thighs
4 bone-in chicken drumsticks
1/4 cup vegetable oil
1/4 cup soy sauce
1/4 cup brown sugar
2 tablespoons lime juice
2 tablespoons orange juice
3 cloves garlic, minced
2 tablespoons fresh ginger, grated
2 tablespoons Caribbean jerk seasoning
1/2 teaspoon allspice
1/2 teaspoon cinnamon
1/2 teaspoon nutmeg
1/2 teaspoon black pepper

1/2 teaspoon cayenne pepper (adjust to taste for spice level)
1/4 cup guava paste, melted
2 tablespoons rum
Instructions:

In a bowl, whisk together vegetable oil, soy sauce, brown sugar, lime juice, orange juice, minced garlic, grated ginger, Caribbean jerk seasoning, allspice, cinnamon, nutmeg, black pepper, and cayenne pepper.

Add the chicken pieces to a large resealable plastic bag and pour the marinade over the chicken. Seal the bag and massage the marinade into the chicken. Refrigerate for at least 4 hours or overnight for the best flavor.

Preheat the grill to medium-high heat and lightly oil the grate.

Remove the chicken from the marinade and let any excess drip off. Reserve the marinade.

Grill the chicken, turning occasionally and basting with the reserved marinade, until the chicken is cooked through and juices run clear, about 30-35 minutes.

In a small saucepan, melt the guava paste over low heat. Stir in the rum and simmer for a few minutes until the flavors meld together.

Brush the grilled chicken with the guava-rum glaze and continue grilling for an additional 2-3 minutes, allowing the glaze to caramelize slightly.

Once done, transfer the Caribbean jerk BBQ chicken

to a serving platter and garnish with fresh cilantro or sliced scotch bonnet peppers for an extra kick.

Serve the succulent and flavorful Caribbean jerk BBQ chicken with your favorite Caribbean-inspired sides and enjoy the vibrant and spicy flavors of this island-inspired dish.

This Caribbean jerk BBQ chicken recipe captures the essence of Caribbean flavors, combining the aromatic spices of jerk seasoning with the sweet and tangy notes of guava and rum, resulting in a delicious and memorable barbecue experience.

TWENTY-THREE

WALTER'S BARBECUE DRY RUB

Ingredients:
1/4 cup brown sugar
2 tablespoons paprika
1 tablespoon chili powder
1 tablespoon garlic powder
1 tablespoon onion powder
1 teaspoon ground cumin
1 teaspoon ground black pepper
1 teaspoon cayenne pepper (adjust to taste)
1 teaspoon dried oregano
1 teaspoon salt

Steps:

In a mixing bowl, combine the brown sugar, paprika, chili powder, garlic powder, onion powder, cumin, black pepper, cayenne pepper, oregano, and salt.

Use a whisk or fork to thoroughly mix the ingredients until well combined and the brown sugar is evenly distributed.

Store the barbecue dry rub in an airtight container or jar until ready to use.

This versatile barbecue dry rub is perfect for seasoning a variety of meats before grilling or smoking, adding a delicious blend of smoky, sweet, and spicy flavors to your favorite cuts of meat.

I hope you enjoy experimenting with this barbecue dry rub to enhance the flavors of your grilled or smoked dishes!

TWENTY-FOUR

WALTER'S BARBECUE CORN

Ingredients:
4 ears of fresh corn, husks removed
2 tablespoons of butter
2 tablespoons of barbecue seasoning
1/4 cup of grated parmesan cheese
Freshly chopped cilantro for garnish
Lime wedges for serving

Steps:
Preheat the grill to medium-high heat.
Brush each ear of corn with melted butter, then sprinkle with barbecue seasoning, ensuring it's evenly coated.
Place the seasoned corn on the grill and cook for 10-12 minutes, turning occasionally, until the kernels are tender and slightly charred.

Once the corn is grilled to perfection, remove it from the heat and transfer to a serving platter.

Sprinkle the grilled corn with grated parmesan cheese and garnish with freshly chopped cilantro.

Serve the barbecue corn with lime wedges on the side for squeezing over the corn before enjoying.

This unique barbecue corn recipe offers a delightful combination of smoky, savory, and slightly spicy flavors, making it a perfect addition to any barbecue gathering or as a standout side dish.

TWENTY-FIVE

WALTER'S BARBECUE BRISKET

Ingredients:
1 whole beef brisket (approximately 10-12 pounds)
1/4 cup brown sugar
2 tablespoons smoked paprika
2 tablespoons garlic powder
2 tablespoons onion powder
1 tablespoon ground cumin
2 teaspoons chili powder
2 teaspoons black pepper
1 teaspoon cayenne pepper
1 teaspoon dried oregano
1 teaspoon salt
2 cups beef broth
1 cup barbecue sauce
Steps:

Preheat your smoker or grill to 250°F (120°C) using hickory or mesquite wood for a rich smoky flavor.

In a small bowl, mix together the brown sugar, smoked paprika, garlic powder, onion powder, cumin, chili powder, black pepper, cayenne pepper, oregano, and salt to create the dry rub.

Rub the brisket generously with the dry rub, ensuring it's evenly coated on all sides. Let it sit at room temperature for 30 minutes to allow the flavors to penetrate the meat.

Place the seasoned brisket on the smoker or grill, close the lid, and let it smoke for 6-8 hours, or until the internal temperature reaches 195-205°F (90-95°C).

Once the brisket reaches the desired temperature, remove it from the smoker and tightly wrap it in aluminum foil. Allow it to rest for 1-2 hours to let the juices redistribute.

In a saucepan, heat the beef broth and barbecue sauce over medium heat to create a basting liquid.

Unwrap the brisket and brush it with the basting liquid, then return it to the smoker or grill for an additional 30-60 minutes to set the glaze.

Once done, remove the brisket from the heat and let it rest for another 15-20 minutes before slicing it against the grain.

Serve the tender, succulent barbecue brisket with your favorite sides and extra barbecue sauce on the side.

This barbecue brisket recipe results in a perfectly

smoked and flavorful dish that's sure to impress your guests and elevate any barbecue gathering!

TWENTY-SIX

WALTER'S BARBECUE CHICKEN TENDERS

Ingredients:
1 lb chicken tenders
1 cup buttermilk
1 cup all-purpose flour
1 teaspoon paprika
1 teaspoon garlic powder
1 teaspoon onion powder
1 teaspoon cayenne pepper
1 teaspoon salt
1/2 teaspoon black pepper
1 cup barbecue sauce
Vegetable oil for frying
Steps:

In a bowl, marinate the chicken tenders in buttermilk for at least 30 minutes.

In a separate bowl, mix the all-purpose flour, paprika, garlic powder, onion powder, cayenne pepper, salt, and black pepper to create the seasoned flour mixture.

Heat vegetable oil in a deep skillet or frying pan over medium-high heat.

Dredge the buttermilk-soaked chicken tenders in the seasoned flour mixture, ensuring they are evenly coated.

Carefully place the coated chicken tenders into the hot oil and fry until golden brown and crispy, about 4-5 minutes per side.

Once the chicken tenders are cooked through and crispy, remove them from the oil and place them on a paper towel-lined plate to drain any excess oil.

In a separate bowl, warm the barbecue sauce in the microwave or on the stovetop.

Toss the fried chicken tenders in the warmed barbecue sauce until they are evenly coated.

Serve the crispy barbecue chicken tenders with extra barbecue sauce for dipping and enjoy the delicious combination of crispy, savory, and tangy flavors.

I hope you enjoy making and savoring these crispy barbecue chicken tenders! If you have any other requests or need further assistance, feel free to ask at waltertheeducator.com.

TWENTY-SEVEN

WALTER'S BARBECUE EGGPLANT WITH MINT AND FETA

Ingredients:
2 medium-sized eggplants
1/4 cup olive oil
2 cloves garlic, minced
2 tablespoons balsamic vinegar
1 teaspoon smoked paprika
1 teaspoon cumin
Salt and pepper to taste
1/4 cup crumbled feta cheese
Fresh mint leaves, chopped for garnish
Instructions:
Preheat the grill to medium-high heat.
Cut the eggplants into 1/2-inch thick slices. In a

small bowl, whisk together the olive oil, minced garlic, balsamic vinegar, smoked paprika, cumin, salt, and pepper.

Brush the eggplant slices with the olive oil mixture on both sides.

Place the eggplant slices on the preheated grill and cook for about 4-5 minutes on each side, or until they develop grill marks and become tender.

Once the eggplant is cooked, transfer it to a serving platter.

Sprinkle the crumbled feta cheese over the grilled eggplant slices and garnish with freshly chopped mint leaves.

Serve the barbecue eggplant as a delicious and flavorful side dish or as a vegetarian main course.

This barbecue eggplant recipe offers a delightful combination of smoky flavors, tangy balsamic, and the freshness of mint and feta, making it a standout dish for any barbecue or gathering. Enjoy!

TWENTY-EIGHT

WALTER'S BARBECUE BACON WRAPS

Ingredients:
12 slices of bacon
12 small chunks of pineapple
12 large shrimp, peeled and deveined
1/2 cup of your favorite barbecue sauce
Wooden skewers, soaked in water for 30 minutes
Steps:
Preheat your grill to medium-high heat.
Cut each bacon slice in half and place a chunk of pineapple and a shrimp at one end of each half slice.
Roll the bacon tightly around the pineapple and shrimp, then secure with a wooden skewer.
Brush the bacon wraps with barbecue sauce, ensuring they are evenly coated.
Place the bacon wraps on the preheated grill and cook

for 5-7 minutes per side, or until the bacon is crispy and the shrimp is cooked through, basting with more barbecue sauce as needed.

Once done, remove the bacon wraps from the grill and let them rest for a few minutes before serving.

This barbecue bacon wraps recipe offers a delicious combination of smoky bacon, sweet pineapple, succulent shrimp, and flavorful barbecue sauce, making it a crowd-pleasing appetizer or party snack. Enjoy!

TWENTY-NINE

WALTER'S BARBECUE SEAFOOD SKEWERS

Ingredients:
1 pound large shrimp, peeled and deveined
1 pound scallops
1 pound salmon fillets, cut into chunks
1 red bell pepper, sliced
1 yellow bell pepper, sliced
1 red onion, sliced
2 cloves garlic, minced
1/4 cup olive oil
1/4 cup barbecue sauce
2 tablespoons lemon juice
1 teaspoon paprika
1 teaspoon cayenne pepper
Salt and pepper to taste

Chopped fresh parsley for garnish
Steps:

In a large bowl, whisk together the olive oil, barbecue sauce, lemon juice, minced garlic, paprika, cayenne pepper, salt, and pepper to create the marinade.

Add the shrimp, scallops, salmon chunks, sliced bell peppers, and red onion to the marinade, ensuring the seafood and vegetables are evenly coated. Let marinate for 30 minutes.

Preheat the grill to medium-high heat.

Thread the marinated seafood, bell peppers, and onion onto skewers, alternating between the different ingredients.

Place the skewers on the preheated grill and cook for 3-4 minutes on each side, or until the seafood is cooked through and has grill marks.

Once done, remove the skewers from the grill and transfer to a serving platter.

Garnish the barbecue seafood skewers with chopped fresh parsley and serve hot.

This original barbecue seafood recipe promises a delightful blend of smoky, spicy, and savory flavors, making it a perfect addition to any barbecue gathering or special occasion. Enjoy the delicious taste of grilled seafood!

ABOUT THE AUTHOR

Walter the Educator is one of the pseudonyms for Walter Anderson. Formally educated in Chemistry, Business, and Education, he is an educator, an author, a diverse entrepreneur, and he is the son of a disabled war veteran. "Walter the Educator" shares his time between educating and creating. He holds interests and owns several creative projects that entertain, enlighten, enhance, and educate, hoping to inspire and motivate you.

Follow, find new works, and stay up to date
with Walter the Educator™
at WaltertheEducator.com

www.ingramcontent.com/pod-product-compliance
Lightning Source LLC
LaVergne TN
LVHW052002060526
838201LV00059B/3795